REMEMBER ME

Torn Curtain Publishing
Wellington, New Zealand
www.torncurtainpublishing.com

© Copyright 2022 Adrian Gomez. All rights reserved.

ISBN Softcover 978-0-473-65759-8
ISBN Hardcover 978-0-473-65760-4
ISBN Epub 978-0-473-65761-1

No portion of this book may be reproduced, stored in a retrieval system or transmitted in any form or by any means—electronic, mechanical, photocopy, recording or otherwise—except for brief quotations in printed reviews or promotion, without prior written permission from the author.

Unless otherwise noted, all scripture is taken from the New International Version®, NIV®. Copyright © 1973, 1978, 1984, 2011 by Biblica, Inc.™ Used by permission of Zondervan. All rights reserved worldwide.

Scripture quotations marked NLT are taken from the New Living Translation, copyright © 1996, 2004, 2015 by Tyndale House Foundation. Used by permission of Tyndale House Publishers, Inc., Carol Stream, Illinois 60188. All rights reserved.

Scripture quotations marked TPT are from The Passion Translation®. Copyright © 2017, 2018, 2020 by Passion & Fire Ministries, Inc. Used by permission. All rights reserved. ThePassionTranslation.com.

Scripture quotations marked TLB are taken from The Living Bible, copyright © 1971 by Tyndale House Foundation. Used by permission of Tyndale House Publishers, Carol Stream, Illinois 60188. All rights reserved.

Scripture quotations marked NKJV are taken from the New King James Version®. Copyright © 1982 by Thomas Nelson. Used by permission. All rights reserved.

Scripture quotations marked ESV are from the ESV® Bible (The Holy Bible, English Standard Version®), copyright © 2001 by Crossway, a publishing ministry of Good News Publishers. Used by permission. All rights reserved.

Scripture quotations marked NASB are taken from the New American Standard Bible®, Copyright © 1960, 1971, 1977, 1995, 2020 by The Lockman Foundation. Used by permission. All rights reserved. www.lockman.org

Scripture quotations marked MSG are taken from THE MESSAGE, copyright © 1993, 2002, 2018 by Eugene H. Peterson. Used by permission of NavPress. All rights reserved. Represented by Tyndale House Publishers, a Division of Tyndale House Ministries.

Cataloguing in Publishing Data
  Title: Remember Me
  Author: Adrian Gomez
  Subjects: Christian life and practice, worship; communion, church sacraments, miracles and healing.

A copy of this title is held at the National Library of New Zealand.

REMEMBER ME

Discovering the miracle-working power of Holy Communion

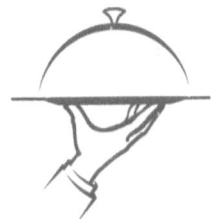

ADRIAN GOMEZ

FOREWORD

It is truly a privilege and joy to write the foreword for not only a faithful and dear friend, but a mentor and spiritual father. Adrian, I honour and thank you for saying 'yes' to God in writing this volume. I read and then re-read *Remember Me* with an ever-deepening sense of anticipation and expectation as to what this book, this act of obedience and faith, could unlock in the hearts and lives of each reader.

Remember Me is an enthralling read that simply, and yet profoundly, introduces you to the power that is to be found in taking Holy Communion. As you flip the pages of this book, the notion of communion as a somewhat infrequent (and even powerless!) church ritual is completely shattered. Instead, you discover a glorious and wonderful invitation for you to come, for you to remember and for you to receive.

Come to a place of deep intimacy and beauty. Remember the ultimate price that was paid as an unfathomable love was poured out for each one of us at Calvary. Receive all that Jesus has purchased for us at the Great Exchange.

This is not a book of dry theological rhetoric; it is a book that unveils a wondrous Truth. A Truth we all need to be reminded of—and engage with. A Truth that will truly set us free.

My deepest desire and prayer is that *Remember Me* will become a well-read companion on countless coffee tables across the globe. When these words translate to action, it will be the beginning of an intimate and powerful relationship with our Creator God.

How marvellous that the King of Glory would bid us 'come'. I for one will gladly enter in. The invitation of this book is: Will you?

Adrian, I know that this is simply the first fruit of many books God is birthing in your heart. I look forward to the next one!

SHALOM!

Dr MJ Swan

> *For as often as you eat this bread and*
> *drink this cup, you proclaim the Lord's*
> *death till He comes. 1 Cor. 11:26 (NKJV)*

CONTENTS

Foreword	v
Preface: Creative Miracles	1
PART ONE: COME	**5**
Chapter 1 *God's Masterpiece*	7
Chapter 2 *God's Restoration*	11
Chapter 3 *God's Reinstatement*	15
PART TWO: REMEMBER	**19**
Chapter 4 *Supernatural Bread*	21
Chapter 5 *Power in the Shed Blood*	27
Chapter 6 *Discerning His Body*	33
PART THREE: RECEIVE	**41**
Chapter 7 *Activating Faith*	43
Chapter 8 *Partaking of Holy Communion*	47
Author's Note: A Hindrance to a Promise	53
Acknowledgements	59
About the Author	61

And without faith living within us, it would be impossible to please God. For we come to God in faith knowing that he is real and that he rewards the faith of those who passionately seek him.

Hebrews 11:6 (TPT)

PREFACE

Creative Miracles

Have you ever seen angels going about their work?

I was standing on the platform of our local church sharing about Holy Communion when I saw it: A stairway had appeared towards the back of the left aisle, and angelic beings from heaven were ascending and descending. They had in their hands dome-shaped trays, and were busy serving people—it was as though we were at a great banquet.

I was curious as to what was under the domes, so I asked God about them. In response, He invited me to look around the room. *See that woman in the third row? She's been given a new heart . . . Oh, and look in the back row! He's just received a set of new eardrums!*

These angels were literally delivering the things people were asking and trusting God for! Across the auditorium, miracles were taking place, yet sadly, I also noticed some angels returning up the stairway with their trays unopened, because the people they had come to serve did not really believe that they could have their healing.

I stood amazed on the platform, realising that no one else was seeing what I was. It was an overwhelming moment as God allowed me to witness these creative miracles. In awe, I thought to myself, *How can this be happening? I didn't even preach!* God knew exactly what I was thinking and said to me, "Son, don't limit yourself to preaching only. People all over the world need to read about and experience the supernatural exchange that takes place when they receive Holy Communion for themselves."

Sometime later, I did a bit of research and came across people who testified of visions and dreams they had received about heaven. Many described seeing large filing rooms lined with cabinets in which brand new body parts were stored in drawers. The drawers were not labelled by body parts, but with people's names. Angelic beings were coming and going out of these rooms carrying what appeared to be named trays with the needed parts on them. The similarities between their visions and the vision I had seen when I led communion strengthened my understanding of creative miracles. God had opened my spiritual eyes to see the splendour of His magnificent power that is ushered in when we reverence and remember Him through Holy Communion.

∼

Writing about the power of communion wasn't something I had ever considered doing, yet through the encouragement of others God faithfully confirmed this assignment. I had often taken communion with a few small groups, and during our time together God's manifest presence was so tangible that people would weep, overcome by what Christ had endured for them on the cross. After one such time of communion, two

PREFACE

individuals approached me to say they had never witnessed anything like it and urged me to write about it so others too could share in this experience. They even offered to pre-purchase the first copies if I turned it into a book!

Spurred on, I began writing an article about the revelation I had received during my vision. But having never before written something for others to read, I quickly found myself in a state of panic—I had no clue as to how to do this! It was clear I needed God's help, so I committed the task to Him and asked the Holy Spirit to guide me. Once I got underway, I found myself writing things I hadn't planned to, and rather than an article, a book started to take shape. The truth of what Proverbs 3:6 teaches became evident to me: If we acknowledge God in our tasks, He will direct our path.

~

One of the reasons I am passionate about sharing Holy Communion with people is because God turns up whenever we reverence Him. I have seen healing miracles in front of my eyes and observed the sheer amazement on people's faces when God shows up and does what He does best. It is not the case that everyone present is always healed, and I do not have all the answers for this. What I do know, is that *you* are valuable to God. You are His very own masterpiece, and if something is not right, He is willing to do whatever is necessary to restore you. Communion is a vital part of that restoration process. The good news is that there is no need to wait—the power of taking the bread and the cup is not confined to a special service but is available to every believer whenever and wherever they break bread in remembrance of Christ.

As you read, I pray you will discover a fresh truth and understanding about this precious gift. I want to activate your faith and equip you to believe God for your own breakthroughs so that you, too, can experience the supernatural exchange of communion and confidently testify: *I have borne witness to creative miracles.*

COME

Come, all you who are thirsty, come to the waters; and you who have no money, come, buy and eat! Come, buy wine and milk without money and without cost. Isaiah 55:1

1

GOD'S MASTERPIECE

His workmanship is marvellous

You are so unique, so wonderfully complex, that God Himself marvels at His workmanship on display through you. He knows how valuable you are even if you cannot yet fully comprehend it. You were miraculously woven together in the privacy of your mother's womb. In that dark secluded space, the hands of God skilfully shaped you from nothing to something. David describes this mysterious process, saying:

You made all the delicate, inner parts of my body and knit them together in my mother's womb. Thank you for making me so wonderfully complex! It is amazing to think about. Your workmanship is marvellous—and how well I know it. You were there while I was being formed in utter seclusion! You saw me before I was born and scheduled each day of my life before I began to breathe. Every day was recorded in your book!

Psalm 139:13-16 (TLB)

Not only are you a manifestation of God's workmanship, you are His masterpiece (Ephesians 2:10)! You are the ultimate demonstration of God's ability, the consummate example of His skill and excellence, the crowning act of His creation. How magnificent is that thought! God intricately and purposefully created you; there is no one like you. This is a truth that Psalm 139:14 invites us to know 'full well'. The question is, *How well is 'full well'?*

I suspect that many of us feel far from the celebrated masterpiece God declares us to be. This can cause us to feel unworthy to partake of communion. To remedy this, let's go back to the beginning and discover God's original intention for His people.

When God created Adam and Eve He said, "Let them have dominion…over all the earth" (Genesis 1:26, ESV). Likewise, we read, "The heaven, *even* the heavens, *are* the LORD's; but the earth he has given to the children of men" (Psalm 115:16, NKJV). From the outset of creation, God invited His children to operate in their God-given authority, co-reigning with Him as royal sons and daughters. What a privilege!

Of course, Satan was vehemently opposed to this display of God's workmanship. The enemy knew that if Adam and Eve—and every subsequent generation—lived out their God-given destiny, he would lose his foothold on earth. Quickly, he intervened. Entering the Garden of Eden, he tempted Adam and Eve to sin by disobeying God.

God had told Adam and Eve they could eat of any tree in the garden except for one, saying, "But of the tree of the knowledge of good and evil you shall not eat, for in the day that you eat of it you shall surely die" (Genesis 2:17, NKJV). Satan manipulated God's Word, assuring Adam and Eve that they would not die, but instead would become 'like God' (Genesis 3:4-5). Taking the fruit he offered them, they embarked on the pursuit of wisdom apart from God. In that moment, the Creator's image in them was marred, and their disobedience caused all humanity to become separated from God. Spiritually cut off, they were expelled from the garden, and instead of walking in blessing and intimacy, they came under the curse of sin . . . its penalty, death.

Today, the enemy continues with his relentless distractions and deceptions. He is well-acquainted with God's Word and he does not wish for us to walk in fullness of its revelation. So, he lies to us, sowing seeds of doubt into our hearts and minds about who God is and what He has said. This is in keeping with his character; for as the apostle John tells us, "He is a liar and the father of lies" (John 8:44). In contrast, God is a covenant-keeping God, meaning that He cannot and will not go back on His word, because that would make Him a liar, and "God is not a man that he should lie" (Numbers 23:19, NKJV). God is trustworthy and therefore His word is also.

The Bible warns us to be familiar with Satan's schemes so that he is not able to outsmart us (2 Corinthians 2:11). But in order to recognise his ploys, we must be relentless in our pursuit of truth. God made it abundantly clear how important this pursuit is when He declared, "My people are destroyed for lack of knowledge" (Hosea 4:6, NKJV). The knowledge referred to here is the written Word of God, the Bible. We must value the Scriptures, taking the time to become familiar with them so that the enemy is not able to manipulate them and use them as a weapon against us as he did with Eve.

Jesus made it clear that when we know the truth, the truth will set us free (John 8:32). The truth that He spoke of, was Himself. Jesus is the Living Word, the One to whom the Scriptures constantly point. If you find yourself at a crossroads in your life, there is only one road that leads to truth *and* to restoration: Jesus. Choose Him! Don't allow yourself to lose heart. Remember, there is still hope! Satan may have taken our authority in the Garden of Eden when he tricked Eve into wilfully giving it to him, but Jesus has reclaimed it once and for all, and He now invites us to share in it with Him.

God knows the plans He has for you—He has even written a book about *your* life! Psalm 139 reminds us of this reality: "You saw who you created me to be before I became me! *Before I'd ever seen the light of day*, the number of days you planned for me were already recorded in your book" (v. 16, TPT).

You are not reading these words by accident or coincidence, but rather by divine appointment. God wants you to discover the plans He has purposed for you and to walk in the authority He always intended for you to possess, so you can uncover the masterpiece you truly are. Partaking in Holy Communion will play a pivotal role in that process, enabling you to realise the full extent of what Jesus has purchased for you on the cross.

2

GOD'S RESTORATION

I have come that they might have life and have it to the full

Prior to Christ's crucifixion we were doomed and condemned. Adam and Eve's sin had become our own, and we were guilty in the eyes of God. There was no escaping the wages of sin: Death. It seemed like a hopeless situation, but God had a plan to set us free from this penalty and to restore us in His image. That plan was the cross.

The cross was the reason He sent His one and only Son, and the means by which He released us from condemnation and saved us for Himself. As Jesus hung upon that cross and declared, "It is finished," He was announcing to the world that Satan's hold was over. The price had been paid—no longer could he steal, kill, and destroy God's children. Jesus had made the abundant life possible (John 10:10)!

Because of the cross, the promises and blessings of God are now available to those who come into a relationship with

Him through the blood of His Son, Jesus Christ. However, if we are to enter into this new life, we must first acknowledge that we are broken and in need of restoration. In 1 John we read:

> *If we walk in the light as he is in the light, we have fellowship with one another, and the blood of Jesus Christ his Son cleanses us from all sin. If we say we have no sin, we deceive ourselves, and the truth is not in us. If we confess our sins, he is faithful and just to forgive us our sins and to cleanse us from all unrighteousness.*
>
> **1 John 1:7-9 (ESV)**

When we admit our sins to God, the blood of Jesus provides complete forgiveness. According to Hebrews 10, those who are cleansed by His blood have been made perfect (v. 14). This is the kindness of God toward us—that He purchased our freedom with the blood of His beloved Son (Ephesians 2:7).

The apostle Paul tells us that in order to receive this extravagant gift of grace, all we need to do is to declare with our mouths that Jesus is Lord and believe in our hearts that God raised Him from the dead. "For it is with your heart that you believe and are justified, and it is with your mouth that you profess your faith and are saved" (Romans 10:9-10).

If you have not experienced this salvation, I would like to invite you into your own personal relationship with God Almighty. When you enter into relationship with Him, your spirit is reborn. It was dead, cut off as a consequence of Adam and Eve's sin in the Garden of Eden, but when you receive Jesus as your Saviour, it comes to life again. More than that, you actually become the Lord's temple—the Holy Spirit Himself resides in you and helps you live out the calling and purpose God has for your life.

Though we cannot fully comprehend God, when we accept Him to be Lord of our lives, His Spirit within us gives us a profound understanding of Him and His ways; He becomes real to us. And the more time we spend with Him, reading the Bible as His love letter to us, the more intimate our relationship becomes. As we draw near, He reveals His plans and purposes for our lives, inviting us to partner with Him to make the world a better place. He longs to see all creation restored!

If you would like to invite Jesus into your heart, here is a prayer to help you do so:

> *"Father God, I believe that Jesus Christ is Your only begotten Son who came to the earth in flesh and died a gruesome death on the cross for my sins. I believe that Jesus rose again on the third day, ascended into heaven, and is seated at Your right hand. Please forgive me for the things I have done that were not pleasing in Your sight and wash away all my sins. Thank You for giving me the gift of eternal life through the blood of Jesus and for giving me a fresh start. I ask You to come into my heart and to be my Lord and Saviour. In Jesus' name, Amen."*

If you have prayed this prayer sincerely, you are now born again—not because of your own works, but because of His. You have been saved by grace through faith, and the confidence you now have is that when God starts something in you, He promises to finish it. Welcome to the family of God!

As you start out on your faith journey, I encourage you to find a church that teaches the Bible. The Christian life is designed to be enjoyed with others. The Bible is filled with verses that exhort us to love one another, serve one another, encourage one another, and pray for one another. Each of these commands requires us to be in relationship with other Christians. Prioritising connection with other believers will help you mature and grow into the fullness God has for you, and is an important part of the restoration process. It is in community with God *and* His people that we discover our purpose.

3

GOD'S REINSTATEMENT

We reflect the glory of the Lord

By definition, 'restoration' means returning something back to its original condition. But when God restores, the result is greater than the original condition because His goal is to take us from 'strength to strength' and 'glory to glory' (2 Corinthians 3:18). God's redemptive work in our lives is the ultimate example of His excellence. He goes beyond merely setting us free from sin, and invites us to partner with Him once again as royal sons and daughters.

In other words, God not only restores us to what He intended, He also reinstates us for a greater purpose! Ephesians 2 makes it clear that He has assignments for each of us. In the Amplified Bible we read:

For we are His workmanship [His own master work, a work of art], created in Christ Jesus [reborn from above— spiritually transformed, renewed, ready to be used] for good works, which God prepared [for us] beforehand [taking paths which He set], so that we would walk in them [living the good life which He prearranged and made ready for us].

Ephesians 2:10 (AMP)

How amazing it is to discover the purpose for your life here on earth! It follows, however, that if you do not know why you are here or what you were born to accomplish, you will struggle to understand or fulfil your purpose.

Let's put it in simple terms: If you see an interesting gadget in the department store and decide to buy it, even though you don't really understand its purpose, what do you do? Would you not contact the manufacturer—the creator—of that gadget and find out what its actual purpose is? The manufacturer will not only tell you why it was created, but will also give you a user manual outlining all there is to know about how that gadget operates.

God is your manufacturer, your creator, and your source of power. He longs for you to come into His presence and spend time with Him. He wants to tell you why He created you, the giftings He has placed in you, and what your purpose is here on earth. In Jeremiah 29:11 He declares, "For I know the plans I have for you, plans to prosper you and not to harm you, plans to give you hope and a future."

God wants you to read His Word and understand His plans for your life. Discovering such wisdom is like finding hidden treasure. The apostle Paul writes:

> *As it is written: "Eye has not seen, nor ear heard, nor have entered into the heart of man the things which God has*

> *prepared for those who love Him." But God has revealed them to us through His Spirit. For the Spirit searches all things, yes, the deep things of God. For what man knows the things of a man except the spirit of the man which is in him? Even so no one knows the things of God except the Spirit of God.*
>
> **1 Corinthians 2:9-11 (NKJV)**

With the Holy Spirit as your teacher and guide, you have the power to unlock mysteries in the heavenly realm and fully live out God's purposes for you.

Remember, you are made in God's image and likeness. You are extraordinarily precious to Him! He delights in prospering His people and reinstating them to the glory He intended. There is no room for us to take pride in our elevated status. Instead, we must allow humility and righteousness to govern our lives. In so doing, others will recognise that our true value is a reflection of Him, and He will receive all the glory.

REMEMBER

After taking the cup, he gave thanks and said, "Take this and divide it among you. For I tell you I will not drink again from the fruit of the vine until the kingdom of God comes." And he took bread, gave thanks and broke it, and gave it to them, saying, "This is my body given for you; do this in remembrance of me." Luke 22:17-19

4

SUPERNATURAL BREAD

He gave thanks and broke the loaves

The Bible tells of an occasion when Jesus, grieving the death of his cousin and herald, John the Baptist, tried to retreat to a solitary place. However, the crowds followed Him, and seeing nightfall fast approaching, the disciples suggested it was perhaps time to send them on their way so they could reach the surrounding villages in time to purchase food. To their amazement, Jesus replied, "They do not need to go away. You give them something to eat" (Matthew 14:16).

What happened next was utterly miraculous! Let's read the exchange between Jesus and His disciples:

"We have here only five loaves of bread and two fish," they answered. "Bring them here to me," he said. And he directed the people to sit down on the grass. Taking the five loaves and the two fish and looking up to heaven, he gave thanks and broke the loaves. Then he gave them to the disciples, and the disciples gave them to the people.

They all ate and were satisfied, and the disciples picked up twelve basketfuls of broken pieces that were left over. The number of those who ate was about five thousand men, besides women and children.

Matthew 14:16-21

Jesus took the little that the disciples had and multiplied it to meet the needs of the people before Him! Interestingly, this wasn't the only time that Jesus supernaturally fed the masses. On another occasion, when He was in Galilee, he climbed up a mountainside, and we're simply told that He sat down. Then, from that position of rest, He proceeded to heal the crowds who flocked to Him. But once again, dinnertime became an issue. This time, Jesus turned to His disciples and said:

"I have compassion for these people; they have already been with me three days and have nothing to eat. I do not want to send them away hungry, or they may collapse on the way."

Matthew 15:32

The disciples were not sure how they could help, so they asked Him, "Where could we get enough bread in this remote place to feed such a crowd?" (v. 33). But Jesus wasn't worried about what they didn't have; He just wanted to know what they *did* have!

"How many loaves do you have?" Jesus asked. "Seven," they replied, "and a few small fish." He told the crowd to sit down on the ground. Then he took the seven loaves and the fish, and when he had given thanks, he broke them and gave them to the disciples, and they in turn to the people. They all ate and were satisfied. Afterward, the disciples

picked up seven basketfuls of broken pieces that were left over. The number of those who ate was four thousand men, besides women and children.

Matthew 15:34-38

Once again, we see God's miraculous power at work. In both situations, God supernaturally fed thousands with only a few loaves of bread and a few small fish.

Can you imagine what this was like for the disciples? They knew the impossibility of providing for so many people with the little they had in their hands. Yet Jesus took what they had to offer and, looking up to heaven, gave thanks to God before giving it back to the disciples to feed the people. When the twelve disciples acted on Jesus' instructions and under His authority, the little became much!

Jesus was teaching His disciples and the crowd about how God provides. This is still true today. If you will present what you have to God—no matter how insignificant it seems—and act in the authority that has been given to you through Jesus, He brings multiplication and increase. Give Him thanks for what you do have, and ask Him to bless it. Not only will what you have overflow into the lives of others, but you, too, will be satisfied. This is a lesson in itself. But there is another lesson Scripture teaches us about bread and it is this: *Bread has the power to sustain life.*

It is interesting that when Coronavirus led to a global pandemic, some of the first foods to be cleared from the supermarket racks were bread, flour, and yeast. Since ancient days, the wonderfully complex human body has been sustained and delighted by something as simple and basic as *bread*. When the Israelites wandered in the desert for forty years, it was bread that God rained down to feed and nourish them. This was no ordinary bread, however. It was literally "bread from heaven" (Exodus 16:4). Supernatural in its origin, it pointed the Israelites to their true source of life, their true provider, and ultimately, it pointed them to Jesus.

The bread that fed the five thousand that day on the hillside was meant to do likewise, yet the people failed to understand what was really happening. Hungry for more, they followed Jesus to the other side of the lake, where He dialogued with them, answering their questions and trying to turn their attention to the "food which endures to everlasting life" (John 6:27). We read His words: "Truly, truly, I say to you, it is not Moses who has given you the bread out of heaven, but it is my Father who gives you the true bread out of heaven. For the bread of God is that which comes down out of heaven and *gives life to the world*" (John 6:32-33, NASB).

Then, leaving no room for any doubt in their minds, Jesus declared, "I am the bread of life!" (v. 35). The bread Jesus had broken and miraculously multiplied the previous day had been a physical sign to them that the true *Bread of Life* was now in their midst. But unlike those loaves offered up by a young boy, those who chose to eat this bread—to eat 'His flesh'—would never hunger again (v. 35). Indeed, those who eat the bread Jesus offers will never die (v. 51).

∼

Jesus still feeds the world miraculously with the bread of His body—through Holy Communion. When the apostle Paul was giving instructions to the early Church on how to share in the Lord's Supper, he said:

> *For I received from the Lord that which I also delivered to you: that the Lord Jesus on the same night in which He was betrayed took bread; and when He had given thanks, He broke it and said, "Take, eat; this is My body which is broken for you; do this in remembrance of Me."*
>
> **1 Corinthians 11:23-24 (NKJV)**

Today Jesus invites us to eat the bread of communion in remembrance of Him. I have witnessed time and time again that as we participate in this act of remembrance, breaking the bread, offering it to God in prayer, and asking Him to bless it, it takes on a miraculous dimension to heal every sickness and disease. The bread of communion brings life to our bodies, but even more than that, it brings life to our spirits as we partake in the life of Christ Himself.

5

POWER IN THE SHED BLOOD

Life is in the blood

In the early nineties, while I was living in South Africa, a visiting speaker from the United States came to our church and preached a message on the power of the blood of Jesus that has stayed with me ever since. In it, he shared a testimony about his dad from back in the days when television was not even heard of. His dad, a farmer and preacher, heard an urgent message broadcast over the radio one afternoon that a swarm of locusts was heading his way, devouring every crop in its path.

Now, this man's crop was close to being ready to harvest, which meant that if the locusts passed through his farm, his livelihood would be gone in an instant. Determined that this would not be the case, he and his wife came together, and by faith, prayed over a can of vegetable oil agreeing that this oil symbolised the precious blood of Jesus. They then got on their tractor and anointed the perimeter of their farm with the oil, declaring that the devourer would not cross the 'bloodline' they had established.

The next morning when he woke up, the speaker's dad went to the kitchen window and looked across his farm and saw everything was still intact. His first thought was that perhaps the radio broadcaster had gotten it wrong and there had been no swarm of locusts headed his way, but he decided to inspect the perimeter of his farm anyway to be sure there was no damage. When he got to the boundary line where the locusts were meant to cross, he could not believe what he saw. Piles of dead locusts, up to a metre high, were all along the perimeter where they had drawn the bloodline. Hallelujah for the miracle-working power of the blood of Jesus!

∼

This story reminds me of the plagues that came upon the Egyptians before the first Passover. After Pharaoh had repeatedly refused to let His people go, God pronounced this judgment upon Egypt saying, "All the firstborn in the land of Egypt shall die, from the firstborn of Pharaoh who sits on his throne, even to the firstborn of the female servant who is behind the handmill, and all the firstborn of the animals" (Exodus 11:5, NKJV).

The final 'plague' was the death of the firstborn. However, the Israelites would be spared this fate if they sacrificed an unblemished lamb and then painted their doorposts and lintels with its blood. Afterwards, they were to eat its flesh as a family until none remained. If they did these things, then when the angel of death saw the blood, he would pass them by and they would be spared destruction (Exodus 12:1-13). But the blood was not only a sign to the angel of death; it was also a sign to the people themselves (v. 13).

When the farmer used vegetable oil, like the blood of the Passover lamb, it was a sign, a symbol representing the blood of Jesus. The power is not in the symbol itself but in our faith in God and in the sufficiency of Christ's sacrifice on our behalf. We no longer need to sacrifice animals for the forgiveness of sins or to obtain divine protection because God allowed His Son, Jesus, the One whom John the Baptist heralded as the "Lamb of God," to lay down His life for us (John 1:29).

∼

We experience the supernatural power of the precious blood of our Lord Jesus Christ when we cease leaning on our intellect, experiences and opinions, and instead simply believe and place our faith in the truth of what God has said. In the words of Hebrews 11:1(TPT):

Now faith brings our hopes into reality and becomes the foundation needed to acquire the things we long for. It is all the evidence required to prove what is still unseen.

To act in faith, we first need to understand what we are placing our faith in. When we take the cup, we declare that our faith is in the finished work of Christ, and in His blood shed for us.

The power of the blood of Christ lies in its purity. Scripture tells us that Jesus, our Passover Lamb, was "without blemish and without spot" (1 Peter 1:19). His blood is pure because of who He is: He is God! In Acts 20:28 (NKJV), Paul cautioned the elders of the church at Ephesus saying, "Take heed to yourselves and to all the flock, among which the Holy Spirit has made you overseers, to shepherd the church of God *which He purchased with His own blood.*"

Scripture is making it clear that the blood Jesus shed was in no way contaminated. For those who wonder how this is possible, it is because Mary was supernaturally impregnated by the power of the Holy Spirit. As a result, Jesus shared none of her human blood. But what's more significant is that during her pregnancy, no blood was exchanged between herself and Jesus. This is because of the placenta. One of the placenta's functions is to prevent the mother's blood from mixing with that of the baby. It does this by acting as an exchange point between the mother and child with nutrients and oxygen passed over by diffusion only, thus ensuring that the maternal and foetal blood circulation systems are completely separate for the entirety of the pregnancy.

Unblemished blood flowed through Jesus' veins. Conceived by the power of the Spirit and without human father, His blood was without the Adamic stain of sin—hallelujah! Because of this, it had the power to redeem us. The previous Levitical system of priests and sacrifices had been unable to do this. Day after day, the priests had offered up sacrifices that could never take away our sin (Hebrews 10:11). But Jesus, our sacrificial Lamb and Great High Priest, offered His own blood, cleansing us and setting us free to serve the living God (Hebrews 9:14). In His death, He proclaimed the words: "It is finished" (John 19:30). And with that one last cry, the message was clear: No further sacrifice was needed. The war against sin and death had been definitively won. His sacrifice was indeed "once for all" (Hebrews 7:27).

Sin, which had entered the world through a 'tree' had been conquered on a 'tree'—the cross of Christ. When Adam and Eve disobeyed God by eating from the tree of the knowledge of good and evil, all of humanity was cut off from God. But now, divine blood and human form combined to redeem God's creation. Hebrews 2:14 tells us, "Since we, God's children, are human beings—made of flesh and blood—he became flesh and blood too by being born in human form; for only as a human being could he die and in dying break the power of the devil who had the power of death" (TLB). Jesus became flesh and died on a tree, breaking the curse of sin by saturating the tree with his own blood, and in doing so, set us free.

We who were dead in sin, are now alive in Christ (Romans 6:11)! There is power in the blood, for life is in it (Leviticus 17:11), and our life has been redeemed by Christ's own blood. Just as the tree was saturated with the blood of Christ, so must our lives be. Only His blood can cleanse us from all sin, wash us clean, and remove sin's crimson stain, leaving us white and pure as snow (1 John 1:7, Revelation 1:5, Isaiah 1:18).

But the blood of Jesus not only cleanses us—it heals us. Both Isaiah 53:5 and 1 Peter 2:24 tell us that we were healed by His stripes. The stripes refer to the injuries Jesus received after being whipped and beaten. The blood that flowed from His open wounds purchased our healing—spiritually *and* physically.

～

The story is told of a doctor by the name of Kent Brantly. Having contracted the Ebola disease, Dr Brantly did not look like he was going to make it. However, he received a blood transfusion from a fourteen-year-old boy who, incidentally, had made a full recovery from Ebola because of Dr Brantly's care. When a patient survives Ebola, antibodies develop in their blood. If that blood is then shared with another person via transfusion, those antibodies work to fight off the virus in the recipient's bloodstream. After receiving such a transfusion, Brantly recovered. He then went on to donate units of his blood to save others who contracted the same illness.

What a picture of the power in the blood to save lives from deadly diseases! When we apply the pure, unblemished blood of Jesus, His blood has power to cleanse us from all sin, to heal us from all sickness and disease, and to deliver us from all the evil works of the devil.

For this reason, after exhorting us to partake of the bread, a symbol of His body, He also invites us to drink the cup of His blood. We read:

In the same way, he took the cup of wine after supper, saying, "This cup is the new agreement between God and you that has been established and set in motion by my blood. Do this in remembrance of me whenever you drink it."

1 Corinthians 11:25 (TLB)

Every time we take the cup, we not only remember the Lord, we also proclaim our faith in what His blood has done for us.

6

DISCERNING HIS BODY

---

*The punishment for our wellbeing
fell on Him*

When we partake of Holy Communion, we remember Jesus' body broken and His blood shed for us. But we also remember His sufferings on our behalf. The agony of the cross was no surprise to Jesus. He knew what He would endure on the cross long before He got to Calvary. On the night He was to be arrested, Jesus retreated to the Garden of Gethsemane where three times He prayed, "My Father, if it is possible *may this cup be taken from me*. Yet not as I will, but as you will" (Matthew 26:39).

Jesus' prayer reveals the depth of His submission to the Father. Knowing the anguish that awaited Him, He said to His Father, "If it is not possible for this cup to be taken away unless I drink it, *may your will be done*" (Matthew 26:42, NLT). Jesus willingly drank the cup of God's wrath so that we could receive the cup of God's grace. It was the greatest sacrifice ever made. Jesus, a righteous and innocent man, was crucified on a cross in our place.

Crucifixion was chosen as a punishment for particularly vicious male criminals. Known for its horrifically slow and painful death, the Roman Senator Cicero described it as, "the most cruel and disgusting penalty; the worst of deaths." In fact, the word 'excruciating' derives its meaning from the Latin root *cruciare*, 'to crucify'. It literally means 'a pain like the pain of crucifixion'.

This excruciating death is what Jesus willingly endured so we could be set free and experience a full and satisfying life. Yet so often we fail to appreciate what Christ went through to purchase our freedom. It was only when I asked the Lord what Paul meant when he cautioned that "those who eat and drink without discerning the body of Christ eat and drink judgment on themselves," that I came to understand the extent of His suffering on my behalf and what it means to 'discern Christ's body' (1 Corinthians 11:29).

First, God showed me the pain of Jesus' scourging. Scourging—or whipping—was not normally a form of execution, but in many cases, it was brutal enough to be fatal. I saw that when Jesus was scourged, He endured a level of torture that was nearly, or perhaps equally, as excruciating as the cross. Stripped of His clothing, Jesus was tied to an upright post. Strong guards stood either side of Him holding whips known as 'flagellum'. Made of leather with pieces of lead and bone inserted into its ends, this instrument was designed to lacerate the skin to the point where even the inner organs would become exposed.

Jesus paid a price far beyond anything we will ever be able to comprehend. He would have been beaten incessantly with those whips, the leather straps wrapping around His shoulders,

His rib cage, His waist, His thighs—every blow ripping His skin and exposing His flesh.

What a moment it was when I realised that I could only experience wholeness because of Jesus' willingness to drink the cup before Him. And the same is true for you.

> *If you are suffering from any physical disorder in your skin or body, especially in your neck, shoulders, spine, kidneys, lower back, buttocks, or thighs, you are healed! Receive it in Jesus' name.*

But their beatings were not confined to His body alone. Matthew 27:28-30 says, "They stripped him and put a scarlet robe on him and made a crown from long thorns and put it on his head and placed a stick in his right hand as a sceptre and knelt before him in mockery. 'Hail, King of the Jews,' they yelled. And they spat on him and grabbed the stick and beat him on the head with it" (TLB).

> *If you have any form of mental illness, brain tumour, or even migraine headaches, the crown upon His brow and those long thorns piercing His scalp deeper and deeper with every blow to the head, were for your healing, you are healed! Receive it in Jesus' name.*

The blows continued until even His eyesight was compromised. Blood streamed down His forehead, flooding His eyes and ears.

> *If you have any sickness in your eyes or ears, He took this upon Himself in exchange for your divine healing, you are healed! Receive it in Jesus' name.*

The crowd punched and kicked Jesus, and they even plucked His beard. It's no wonder the Scripture says, "But many were amazed when they saw him. His face was so disfigured he seemed hardly human, and from his appearance, one would scarcely know he was a man" (Isaiah 52:14, NLT).

If you have any facial disorder, His face was disfigured in exchange for your healing, you are healed! Receive it in Jesus' name.

Weakened from His beating, the pain Jesus endured was incomprehensible, yet still they made Him carry that heavy rugged cross up the Via Dolorosa to Calvary. As He bore that heavy cross on His lacerated back, the burden He carried truly was ours. He felt the weight of all our sin, brokenness and disease. When they finally reached the top of the hill, they stretched Him out on the cross, driving nails through the nerves in His hands to fix Him to it. With every blow of the hammer Jesus would have experienced excruciating pain shooting up from His hands, through His arms and into His torso, causing His hands to tear at the nails as they clawed up in agony.

If you have any disorders in your hands, wrists, elbows, arms, or shoulders, He took your pain on the cross in exchange for divine order and healing, you are healed! Receive it in Jesus' name.

Next, they drove a nail through the nerves of both His feet. Again, excruciating pain would have shot up from His feet through His legs, radiating into His body.

If you have any disorders in your feet, ankles, Achilles tendons, calves, shins, knees, legs, groin, or hips, He took your pain on the cross in exchange for divine healing, you are healed! Receive it in Jesus' name.

The force of the cross crashing down into its place in the ground, caused His limbs to dislocate. Just as the psalmist prophesied hundreds of years earlier, "Every joint in my body has been pulled apart" (Psalm 22:14, MSG).

If you have any disorders or pain in your joints, tendons, ligaments, and cartilage, including arthritis, He took them upon Himself on the cross in exchange for your divine healing, you are healed! Receive it in Jesus' name.

After several hours of this torment, the human heart of Jesus would begin to fail and His lungs collapse. Excess fluids would start to fill the lining of His heart and lungs, adding to the slow process of asphyxiation which primarily affects the cells in the tissue and organs. Deprived of oxygen, these vital cells would begin to die.

If you have any disorders in your heart, your lungs, or any other organ, He took them upon Himself on the cross in exchange for your divine healing, you are healed! Receive it in Jesus' name.

Due to the extreme loss of blood and hyperventilation, Jesus would have then begun to experience severe dehydration. We see this when He cried out, "I thirst" (John 19:28). So intense was this experience that He declared, "My mouth is dried up like a potsherd, and my tongue sticks to the roof of my mouth; you lay me in the dust of death" (Psalm 22:15, NIV). The sour, cheap, vinegar-like wine that was offered to Him was a mockery designed to inflict the final torment. He tasted it but refused to drink it.

> ***If you have any disorders in your mouth, your tongue, or your throat, He took them upon the cross in exchange for your divine healing, you are healed! Receive it in Jesus' name.***

Finally, we hear His words, "It is finished!" Jesus paid in full the debt that had passed from generation to generation since Adam's sin. His mission complete, He bowed His head and released His spirit. We need to understand that when Jesus made this declaration, He took all our sins and sickness, and bore all our diseases unto death in exchange for the divine healing He offers us. In the words of the prophet Isaiah:

> *He was wounded for our transgressions, He was crushed for our wickedness [our sin, our injustice, our wrongdoing]; the punishment [required] for our wellbeing fell on Him, and by His stripes (wounds) we are healed.*
>
> **Isaiah 53:5 (AMP)**

Jesus died to give us what He had promised: *Life in abundance!* (John 10:10).

For this reason, Paul cautions us when we take communion to be sure we discern the body of Christ correctly. When we fail to do so, he says, we "eat and drink judgment on ourselves," or as Eugene Petersen so aptly puts it, "If you give no thought (or worse, don't care) about the broken body of the Master when you eat and drink, you're running the risk of serious consequences" (1 Corinthians 11:29, MSG). Paul goes so far as to say, "That is why many of you are weak and ill, and some have died" (1 Corinthians 11:30, ESV).

Whatever incurable disease you may have, Jesus paid the ultimate price in exchange for your healing. When you partake of Holy Communion, you not only remember His body broken and His blood poured out, you honour His suffering on your behalf and posture yourself to receive its costly fruits.

RECEIVE

For no matter how many promises God has made, they are "Yes" in Christ. And so through him the "Amen" is spoken by us to the glory of God. 2 Corinthians 1:20

7

ACTIVATING FAITH

By His stripes we are healed

I had suffered from lower back pain due to old sports injuries for as long as I could remember. Every morning when I woke, I would sit on the edge of my bed for a while, mentally preparing myself to stand up. Then, when I became a born again Christian, I heard many messages on the subject of Holy Communion. One in particular, by Joseph Prince, revolutionised my understanding of the Lord's Supper. That's when it dawned on me that I had been religiously eating the wafer and sipping the wine every Sunday without truly understanding their significance.

I began taking communion regularly for my back pain, focussing on the exchange Jesus made on the cross for my healing. Initially, when healing did not happen immediately, I struggled with thoughts of doubt and unbelief. I was discouraged and found myself constantly fighting the lies the enemy bombarded me with. Still, I kept declaring healing scriptures over my back as I took communion. Over time, the

Word of God transformed my thought patterns and my faith started growing, until one day I realised the pain in my back was gone! Today, I remain pain-free. Praise God!

I am reminded of the Parable of the Sower in Mark 4. There, Jesus tells a story of a farmer who went out to sow his seed, and as he scattered it, it fell in various places. Some fell along the path only to be eaten by birds, other seeds fell in rocky places where they couldn't take root, and some fell among the thorns where even though they could germinate, the weeds choked out their fruitfulness. Only some seeds fell on good soil, where they were able to bring forth a harvest.

The focus of this parable is more on the soil than the seed because it is the soil that determines whether or not the seed can be fruitful. The soil speaks to the condition of our hearts and our ability to receive God's truth, while the seed represents the Word of God and the message of His Kingdom (Mark 4:14, Matthew 13:19). When our hearts are hardened to that truth, then just as the birds quickly ate the seed that fell on the path, Satan slyly comes and immediately tries to take away the Word that was sown in our hearts (Mark 4:15).

How does he prevent the Word from taking root in our lives? Through deception and lies. Remember, these are his names. He is the Deceiver, and the Father of Lies. These two names speak to the heart of who Satan is and how he behaves. While God sows seeds of truth and hope, the enemy sows seeds of doubt and despair, telling you that your past has made you unworthy to receive healing, or that because the pain is still there, you'll never be healed. If we are to withstand these lies, we must keep believing and declaring the Word of God over our life. There is tremendous power in speaking out the Scriptures. Romans

10:17 tells us that "faith comes by hearing, and hearing by the word of God" (NKJV). As we 'hear' the Word, faith is activated within us, and as faith rises, we are better able to resist the enemy's attempts to steal God's promises from us.

Another way we can stand firm and allow the seed of God's Word to take root in our lives is through submission. In James 4:7 we read, "Submit yourselves therefore to God. Resist the devil, and he will flee from you" (ESV). God does not force us to do anything; we get to choose what we will do. Willingly yielding ourselves to His authority helps protect us from the enemy's schemes. And as we continue to persist in obedience and faith, the enemy must flee.

God wants us to trust that His Word will do what He has said it will. The reason we can have this confidence is because God is not like us—He does not change His mind or fail to act on what He has spoken. God is faithful and always carries out His promises (Numbers 23:19). In fact, Psalm 89 says that every word He speaks is a covenant (v. 34). He binds Himself to His words and He cannot violate them. What's more, God promises us that His words will be fruitful in our lives. As He said to the prophet Isaiah, "So shall My word be that goes forth from My mouth; It shall not return to Me void, but it shall accomplish what I please, and it shall prosper in the thing for which I sent it" (Isaiah 55:11, NKJV).

I dare you to believe His Word—especially what He says about healing! If you had an infection and the doctor prescribed antibiotics to be taken over several days, you would religiously take them without missing a day, *believing what the doctor has told you will work.*

Here's the challenge: *Why not take communion once, twice, even three times a day for your healing, believing that God's Word works?* I am not saying you should discard your medication, but do this as well, and do it often, as Jesus urged us to, believing the truth of Psalm 103:3, that He heals *all* our diseases.

Such faith gets God's attention—in fact, faith is our heavenly currency. This brings us back to Hebrews 11:1(TPT):

> *Now faith brings our hopes into reality and becomes the foundation needed to acquire the things we long for. It is all the evidence required to prove what is still unseen.*

Faith does not look at circumstances, but instead looks to God. It does not listen to people, but trusts God's Word. It dares to trust God to do the impossible, and sees the unseen. However, while faith is the currency of heaven, let me be clear that you cannot 'earn' God's favour with it. Faith is ultimately an expression of love (Galatians 5:6). It is the security of knowing that no matter what, we are deeply loved by the Father. Because we know and love who He is, we can have faith.

The greatest demonstration of God's love for us was portrayed on the cross when, while we were *still sinners*, Christ died for us (Romans 5:6). That unconditional sacrificial love is what we remember and honour every time we receive Holy Communion. Whenever we partake of the Lord's Table, we need to understand it is a holy moment. It is not a ritual to be observed, but a moment in which you participate in the exchange made for you and me on the cross by Jesus Himself. It is a blessing to be received.

Jesus wants us to be discerning of how His body was broken for our healing and wholeness, and conscious of how His blood was shed for our forgiveness.

8

PARTAKING OF HOLY COMMUNION

Draw near to God, and He will draw near to you

As we come to the close of this book, I invite you to partake of Holy Communion, whether by yourself, with your family, or in a group setting. You will need to prepare the following elements: Bread, wafer, matzo, or plain water crackers which symbolise His body, and red juice or sweet red wine which represent His blood. If you do not have red juice or wine, just use water—remember Jesus turned water into wine. The element here is *faith*.

Set the atmosphere and focus on His presence by playing worship music in the background if you can, preferably songs centred around the blood of Jesus. The Bible says that when we worship and reverence Him, coming into His presence with singing, He inhabits our praises (Psalm 22:3). This creates a faith environment where anything is possible. Expect Him to draw near to you as you intentionally draw near to Him (James 4:8).

You can come confidently to this time because you have been granted access to the throne of God, where you can make your requests through the blood of Jesus (Hebrews 10:19). Remember, healing is your portion because of what He endured.

∼

As you get ready to partake in Holy Communion, feelings of doubt and unworthiness can begin to surface. Perhaps you feel hesitant to receive the elements because of Paul's words, "a person must [prayerfully] examine himself [and his relationship to Christ], and only when he has done so should he eat of the bread and drink of the cup. For anyone who eats and drinks [without solemn reverence and heartfelt gratitude for the sacrifice of Christ], eats and drinks a judgment on himself if he does not recognise the body [of Christ]" (1 Corinthians 11:28-29, AMP). If this is you, I want to encourage you with this story:

> *Scottish theologian, John Duncan, was attending a service where communion was being offered. He was personally feeling so defeated and unworthy of partaking, that he allowed the bread and the cup to pass him by. But then he noticed a young girl do the same and he remembered the truth of the Gospel. Leaning forwards, he whispered to her, "Take it, lassie. Take it. It is meant for sinners." And then they took the Lord's Supper together.*

Do not let Christ's sacrifice be in vain! He has made you worthy to receive the elements. Come in full faith that His sacrifice upon the cross was sufficient to allow you to partake in this feast and to freely enter God's presence. But also come in full faith that there is so much more that God wants you to experience: He wants you to walk in healing and wholeness!

Do you remember how doubt caused the angelic beings to return to heaven with creative miracles still intact under their domed trays? Don't let this be your testimony. Instead, be mindful of this holy moment. Discern His body and all that He suffered for you as you ingest His divine healing power. You are healed in Jesus' name.

Let's stretch our faith and come into agreement for the supernatural to happen. *Remember the transfusion Dr Brantly received? And how the antibodies found in another's blood worked to fight off the Ebola virus in his body?* By faith, I believe that when you eat and drink these emblems that symbolise His body and His blood, a blood transfusion will take place. As the wine, juice or water is absorbed into your own bloodstream, any impurities or blood disorders you may have, including leukaemia, must come into divine order. I call every cancerous cell that has conglomerated into a tumour, undetected as a foreign body, and that your blood is feeding, to be be exposed and disintegrate by the power of the pure blood of Jesus. His blood has cleansing power.

In the Word we find numerous occasions when Jesus raised the bread and gave thanks to God for it. It then took on a supernatural dimension. Paul recounts one of these times as he reflects on what God taught him about the last supper:

> *I received from the Lord that which I also delivered to you: that the Lord Jesus on the same night in which*

He was betrayed took bread; and when He had given thanks, He broke it and said, "Take, eat; this is My body which is broken for you; do this in remembrance of Me." In the same manner He also took the cup after supper, saying, "This cup is the new covenant in My blood. This do, as often as you drink it, in remembrance of Me."

1 Corinthians 11:23-25 (NKJV)

∼

Take the bread, which represents the broken body of our Lord Jesus Christ, and raise it up to God. I will start you off in prayer, and you can add to it as He leads you.

"Father God, we ask You to examine our hearts right now and forgive us of every wrong thought, word or deed that has not been pleasing to You. We come humbly before Your throne with thanksgiving in our hearts. We ask You, Father, to bless this bread as we raise it up to You now. We give You thanks and we remember the suffering Jesus' body endured in exchange for our healing, wholeness, and restoration."

Now, take the cup . . .

"Father God, we raise this cup to You. We ask You to bless it, as it represents the precious, unblemished, pure blood of our Lord Jesus Christ shed for our atonement. Thank You, Father, that we can access Your throne of grace through the blood of Jesus. Bless these emblems to our bodies as we partake of them. In Jesus' name we pray, Amen."

PARTAKING OF HOLY COMMUNION

You may go ahead . . . Eat and drink in your own time as you meditate on the powerful exchange Jesus made on the cross for you.

AUTHOR'S NOTE

A Hindrance to a Promise

God is looking for opportunities to work miracles!

Getting started on writing this book was the hardest part of the process for me.

Growing up, I suffered badly from dyslexia. I struggled to form sentences and find the right words, and even when I could, I found it hard to sound them out. This caused me to hate reading. My reading age was well below average, and the other kids would make fun of me, labelling me stupid. It was humiliating, and I feared going to my English classes.

Back then, dyslexia was rarely diagnosed as a learning disability, and because it was left untreated, it had a significant effect on my ability to meet my full potential at school and work. As a child, I began to believe that not only was my inability to read a major obstacle to my learning, but that it might also have long-term educational, social, and economic consequences.

I mention this not so that you can feel sorry for me, but so that you can rejoice with me! There is no limitation God has not already overcome! If I was able to overcome dyslexia by the grace of God and write this book, so can anybody else.

When God said to me, "Son, you need to write about the vision you received," my response was, "You've got to be joking, right? You know that I can't write! I don't even read much." That's when I heard Him say, "Who told you that you can't write?"

At that very moment, the words God asked Adam echoed in my ears, "Who told you, you were naked?" (Genesis 3:11).

I was aware that through this question, the Father was affirming me and inviting me into a journey. Long story short, through the process of writing this book, God identified and challenged the thought patterns which had kept me in bondage for so long, and helped me recognise the deceptive plan of the enemy to steal my ability to write when it was still in seed form.

The devil truly is the father of lies, and he loves to work through people of influence in your world to spread those lies. In my case, he used people in authority, those whom I had the utmost respect for (like my teachers in elementary school), knowing I would believe everything they told me. Back then, when I was told that I was stupid and a failure, my whole academic life took a knock. I lost my confidence to even try. As a result, I turned to sport, where I excelled because of the affirmation I received from my coaches and spectators. Today, my number one love language is 'Words of Affirmation'—no surprises there!

The enemy used similar tactics to try and derail me while I was working on this manuscript. After completing my first draft, I gave it to a close family friend to edit. Bless her heart, she unknowingly stirred up a hornet's nest of negative memories when she returned it with red markings and comments all over the pages. It took me right back to those days in school when the red scratching and negative comments all over my work left me feeling so inadequate and ashamed. My immediate response was, "What was I even thinking? I am not a writer!" I was so angry—even though, of course, my friend had no clue about my past, and her intention was to be helpful, not hurtful. But God used my response to get my attention. He told me, "Son you've got some forgiving to do." I sighed for a moment and realised that God had brought all these things to my memory for a reason—I was about to be liberated into a whole new world of possibilities!

I began to forgive all my teachers, my family members, and even myself for not understanding that I had a learning difficulty. I had to render each of the negative words spoken over my life null and void and declare that they would have no further effect on my life. After doing these things, I asked God to forgive me for believing the lie that I was no good at writing or reading, and for partnering with fear—the fear of failing, of shame, rejection, humiliation and disappointment.

You might want to pause and reflect on your own life here. *Who told you that you were useless at something? Which of your dreams were squashed while they were still in seed form?* Let me encourage you that you do not have to stay stuck in these feelings of failure. When I looked up the meaning of the word 'failure' in a very old Oxford dictionary, to my surprise, it said that failure means 'a hindrance to a promise'. God made us wonderfully complex, and He has a plan for our lives, a plan that will give us hope and a future. The devil knows the Word of

God and will twist it or use it against us to try and derail God's purpose for our lives, because he knows that when we fulfil God's plan, we become a threat to his kingdom of darkness.

To most people, failure when facing major challenges while pursuing their dreams would look like quitting and trying something else. But remember, failure is *only a hindrance to a promise*. Even if you must change course, you do not have to give up on the promise!

To finish this book, I had to change my negative mindsets by believing in the person God created me to be. I have to say, the journey God took me on was rough, and there were times I just wanted to give up. In my own strength, I would never have thought it within my reach to ever write a book. But when I started trusting God with the task, what seemed impossible became possible. I came to a deep understanding that in my weakness, He is strong, His grace is sufficient for me.

God healed the memories that kept me in bondage all those years, and once I chose to forgive, I experienced a freedom which encouraged me to let go of whatever held me back. I began to live with the conviction that I *can* do all things through Christ who strengthens me.

My changed mindset, and beliefs about how God had created me for a purpose, have reprogrammed my brain to believe anything is possible with God. But for this to happen, I had to yield my soul—my mind, will, and emotions—to God and allow Him to be the cultivator, breaking up the ground and uprooting the weeds, so to speak, in my life. Through this cultivation period, God took me through a mental transformation, a mind change led by His Word and His

AUTHOR'S NOTE

Spirit. It took me fifty-six years to realise and believe that the seed was always there, just lying dormant. It took me another five years of conditioning, watered by the Word of God, for the seed to germinate, grow, and bear fruit in its season.

I love how God is no respecter of person. He can use anybody, regardless of their age or ability. Just as He has worked to bring me to a place of purpose and fruitfulness, He will do the same for you.

ACKNOWLEDGEMENTS

Firstly, all glory and honour go to God for the revelation and inspiration and for instructing me to write this book.

Thank you to my wife Ingrid and my New Zealand family for always believing in me and encouraging me over the long five to six-year journey of writing this book. It was Ingrid who encouraged me to take communion with the first group of people just after I received the revelation. Thank you to Martin Swan and Scott Kinley who were in that first group and encouraged me to write about this revelation.

Also thank you to Debbie Swan, who 'edited' my initial article on Holy Communion which stirred up so many negative emotions but also brought so much healing to my old mindsets and beliefs through this journey.

Thank you to Ben Kendrew for giving me some valuable ideas based on his experience as an ex-journalist.

Finally thank you to the team at Torn Curtain Publishing for having my heart through the whole editing process.

ABOUT THE AUTHOR

Adrian Gomez was born in Cape Town, South Africa. He is married to his teenage sweetheart Ingrid and they have two sons who married two beautiful sisters. They have five grandchildren and they all live in New Zealand.

Adrian speaks in churches and facilitates workshops for small groups and ministry teams on the miracle-working power of communion. Adrian and Ingrid are also passionate about building marriages on Biblical foundations, coaching couples and preparing young couples for marriage through their one-day marriage retreats.

To share your testimony or get in touch with Adrian Gomez, please visit:

www.adriangomez.co.nz

www.ingramcontent.com/pod-product-compliance
Lightning Source LLC
LaVergne TN
LVHW091935070526
838200LV00069B/1798